Let's Count Trucks!

A Fun Kids' Counting Book
For Toddler Boys
And Children Age 2 to 5

FREE
Coloring and
Doodle Pages

Alina Niemi

What did you think of this book?

Please consider leaving a review. It helps me get better and helps
others decide if this book will help them. Thank you!

Find more fun books at alinaspencil.com

Plus links to stores with customizable shirts, stickers, mugs, bumper
stickers, personalized pet bowls, phone and laptop cases, custom
photo wall clocks, magnets, greeting cards, and much more!

ISBN: 978-1-937371-03-6

Alina's Pencil Publishing

1 one garbage truck

How many garbage cans do you see?

How many apartment windows can you count?

2 two tow trucks

What happened to the car?

What colors are the trucks?

3 three aerial bucket trucks

How many traffic cones do you see?
What are the workers doing?

4 four tractors

How many cows do you see?
What colors are they?

5 five fire trucks
What are the truck numbers?

6 six forklifts
What do you think they are moving?

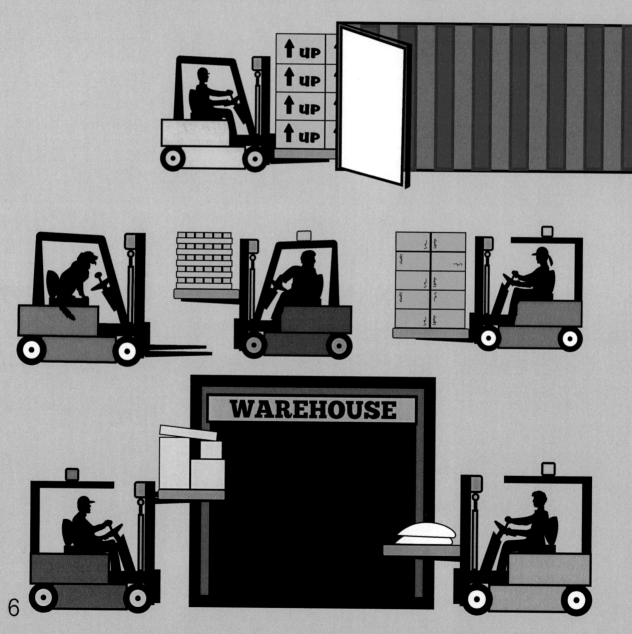

7 seven cement mixers

What colors are they?
How many have stripes?

8 eight delivery trucks
What are they delivering?

9 nine pickup trucks

What colors are they?
How many have trailers?

10 ten food trucks or lunch wagons
What are they selling?
What do you want to eat?

just hot dogs!

MENU
STRAWBERRY
CHOCOLATE
BANANA
MANGO
GUAVA
CUCUMBER

SAIMIN

Waffles
plain
chocolate
jam
syrup

Snacks

Who is driving the forklifts?
What are they moving?

14

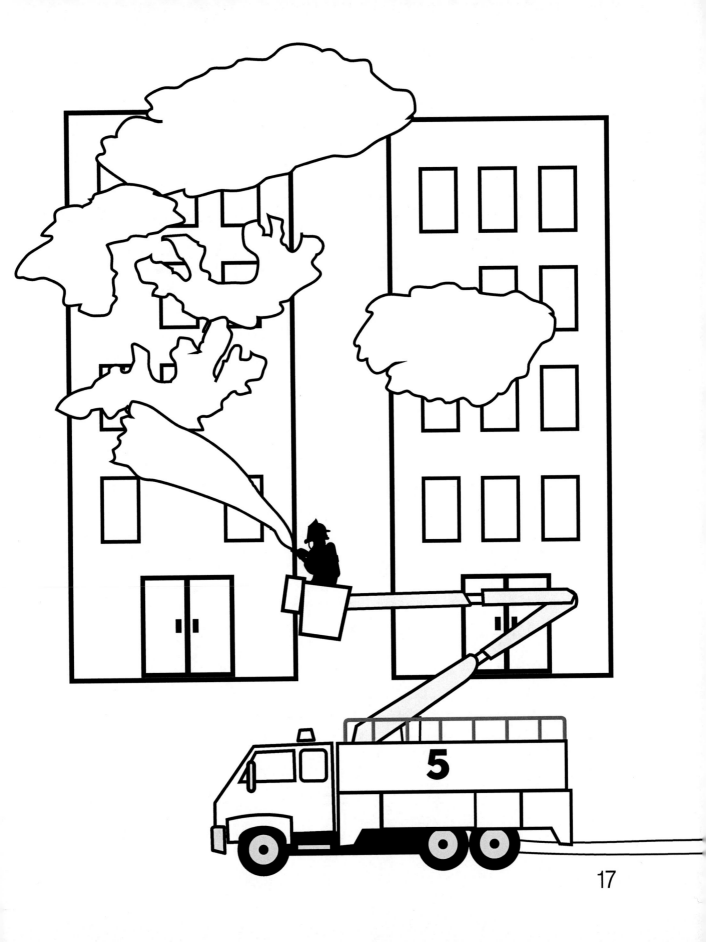

Check out the other books in the series!

Let's Count Summer

Let's Count Summer!

A Fun Kids' Counting Book
For Children Age 2 to 5

Alina Niemi

Teach your children about the seasons and help them recognize different objects they are likely to see.

This book has pages of summer- and beach-themed fun things, such as bathing suits, surfboards, and crabs.

Your child or grandchild can point to each object and count out loud. Many toddlers know their numbers but get confused when counting objects. This is a fun way to practice numbers 1 to 20.

Recommended for children age 2 to 5

Let's Count Halloween

Find favorite Halloween items, like jack-o-lanterns, candy corn, and dancing skeletons. Kids will love the cute pictures and can practice counting numbers 1 to 20.

Recommended for children age 2 to 5

Let's Count Halloween!

A Fun Kids' Counting Book
For Children Age 2 to 5

Alina Niemi

22